INTERIOR
STYLE
maximalism

INTERIOR
STYLE
maximalism

KRISTEN BATEMAN

contents

M ixed, matched and intensely curated, maximalist interior design is incredibly personal and highly individualistic. Prints, vivid colours, unusual items, niche fabrics and unique statement pieces come together to create an entirely uncommon scene. Maximalist interiors span the eras, taking inspiration from all different kinds of time periods, from Victorian and rococo to art deco and beyond. Never just one aesthetic, maximalism originates from any kind of look, feel or time period. Think of it as the closest thing to true personal style in the form of interiors.

This book celebrates maximalist interiors of all kinds. There's the over-the-top ones, with visually charged bursts of colour and prints brought to life, and then there's the more understated visions that bring forwards striking yet subtle details, such as velvet flocking, pink wallpaper and iconic furniture. We start by charting the history of maximalist interiors, using early seventeenth-century Europe as an anchoring point, and leading all the way up to modern times, touching on all the major moments, designers and movements to know. Incorporating iconic elements and showrooms, this book is a tome of endlessly inspiring maximalism that even the more minimal-leaning will find intriguing.

previous page *The interior of Dawnridge, in Beverly Hills, California, the home of the maximalist master Tony Duquette.*

opposite *Madcap Cottage in High Point, North Carolina, is a maximalist take on the English country-house style. Created by Jason Oliver Nixon and John Loecke, who reference Colefax and Fowler and David Hicks among their influences, the dining room is decorated in a pastel palette. The foyer can be seen on page 2.*

Mixed prints! Lush fabrics! Splashy, eccentric and over-the-top colours! Maximalist interior design has been around since the dawn of time and encompasses a 'more is more' aesthetic that is a powerful expression of personality and personal style. Excess and opulence reign supreme and overtake minimalism, typical neutral colourways and conventional furnishings found in homes, bringing forwards a radical vision and vibrant slice of paradise.

Truly, maximalist interiors can be traced back to ancient civilizations and seen throughout all cultures. Certain fabrics or prints, like Paisley or glazed calico, a type of Indian cotton adorned with large florals and botanicals, traces back to the early 1600s. When the Renaissance was at its peak, art was put above all else, heavily influencing interiors going forward. Take, for example, the Château de Chenonceau in Touraine, France, with its current structure built in 1514–22, containing

history

a mix of late Gothic and early Renaissance interiors and architecture. Incredibly influential women resided there over the years, each instilling their own take on maximalist interiors. For example, when the French Queen Catherine de' Medici took over (reigning from 1547–59), she brought with her the Italian Renaissance influence from her native Italy, with enamelled tiles and gilded features. Likewise, the widow Louise de Lorraine's bedroom was painted black and covered in death-like motifs such as tears and gravediggers' shovels.

Maximalism has one of the most extensive and interesting histories of any other genre of interior design. And while it has existed for centuries in one form or another, it's been popular for many reasons. In many cases, over-the-top design represented wealth and status, but today, maximalist interiors are about a powerful act of self-expression more than anything else.

opposite *The opulent bedroom of Catherine de' Medici at the Château de Chenonceau in Touraine, France.*

Baroque

The main rule of maximalist interiors is that there simply are no rules. The design period that really kicked off maximalism was the baroque period. First established in Italy, it quickly spread throughout Europe during the seventeenth century and the first half of the eighteenth century. It was all about gilded details and an overall ornate sense of decorating. Movement, drama and emotion were brought together and put on a grand display in some of the world's most prominent displays at the time: the Church.

Indeed, so wide-ranging was the influence of the maximalist baroque interior that it had a worldwide global influence. According to the Victoria and Albert Museum in London, 'In China, the European pavilions were the grandest expressions of the Qing rulers' interest in the arts of Europe. These European-style palaces were part of the Yuanming Yuan or Old Summer Palace in Beijing, the Emperor Qianlong's summer residence. Designed by Jesuit priests, the pavilions – most of which were completed between 1756 and 1766 – were based on baroque models and included grand fountains and statues.'

Baroque influences can still be seen today on a less extreme level. For one, the baroque interiors often captured a highly dramatic effect with painted ceilings, gold touches and the overdone use of mirrors as a decoration to cover entire walls and large portions of the home. Take, for example, the Royal Palace of Caserta. With construction beginning in 1752, it stood as the former royal residence in Caserta, southern Italy, created as the main seat of the kings of Naples. As the largest palace built in Europe during the eighteenth century, it stands as a whirlwind example of the baroque maximalist interior, complete with the world's best marble, gilded features, pristinely carved statues and richly colourful curtains with lavish decorations throughout. The palace itself includes five floors with 1,200 rooms, 1,742 windows, 34 staircases, 1,026 fireplaces, a large library and a theatre inspired by the Teatro di

opposite *An excellent example of baroque interiors, the Royal Palace of Caserta, Italy, features ornate decorations on the ceilings, walls and marble floors.*

San Carlo of Naples. With all that, the interiors had to match the idea of riches.

Elsewhere, the Palace of Versailles in France is a baroque masterpiece and was reportedly one of the most imitated buildings of the seventeenth century. According to the Victoria and Albert Museum in London, 'In 1717, the Swedish architect Nicodemus Tessin the Younger compiled a "treatise on the decoration of interiors, for all kinds of royal residences, and others of distinction in both town and country", based on his own travel notes. One of the most expensive, recent innovations he recorded was the presence of mirrors so large, they covered entire walls. He also noted the use of glass over the chimney-piece in the King's Chamber at Versailles.'

above *The ceiling of the Hercules Salon on the first floor of the Palace of Versailles in France features the ceiling painting* Apothéose d'Hercule *by François Lemoyne.*

Key to interiors of the baroque era were the combination of beautiful, opulent things put on full display: rare works of colourful art, gold and porcelain and lacquer decorative arts, marble sculptures and even books were proudly displayed as interior decorative *objets*. The baroque home was over the top with respect to furniture too. Take, for example, cabinets with marquetry (layered veneers of differently coloured woods). Flowers and leaves served as central motifs, seen on vases and porcelain objects. By the mid-eighteenth century, tastes turned to simplicity and the overdone look of baroque fell out of style, until it made a reappearance in a different form in the early nineteenth century – but not before rococo was set to make its lasting debut.

above *Colour, print, texture and embellishment mix and match at the Palace of Versailles.*

Rococo

Consider rococo a sister of baroque and one of the foremost influences of maximalist interiors. Exceptionally over the top, rococo was the final movement of the baroque expression, which pulled together all the highly ornamental decoration and made it even more expressive than it already was. Rococo first began in France during the 1720s. What made it different from other design movements of the time was that it was developed by craftspeople and designers rather than architects. The result? Richly decorated furniture and ceramics, silver and other *objets* that covered every surface of the home. Inspired by the French word *rocaille*, which means 'rock' or 'broken shell', these kinds of seaside motif often inspired the designs. Another huge part of the maximalist rococo aesthetic was the acanthus leaf (a symbolic, curly, healing leaf with origins in traditional Greece and Roman design).

The rococo aesthetic in interiors was seen throughout Italy and France, in particular in the royal palaces and churches. Take, for example, the Palazzina di Caccia di Stupinigi, one of the residences of the Royal House of Savoy in northern Italy. It was originally built as a royal hunting lodge in the early eighteenth century, in Stupinigi, a suburb of Nichelino, just south west of Turin. The architect and stage designer Filippo Juvarra (1678–1736) hired a talented team of decorators from Venice to carry out the décor of the palazzina interiors with regal chandeliers, gilded chairs and virtually every surface covered in decorative elements. Anna Caterina Gilli (circa 1700–60) also served as the active decorative painter at the palace.

Similarly, in Paris, there is the Hôtel de Soubise. With pale robin's egg blue walls contrasting against bright gold, the interiors were essential to displaying wealth and power. One

right *The central hall in the Palazzina di Caccia di Stupinigi near Turin, Italy, represents a rococo paradise.*

opposite *The Salon de la Princesse in the Hôtel de Soubise in Paris.*

below *A side table circa 1740, after a design by Matthias Lock, replete with golden details and acanthus details typical of the rococo period.*

.

of the rooms that best represents this is the Salon de la Princesse, an oval-shaped interior embellished in intricate, gilded boiserie (carved wood), cherubs, frescos and an exceptional number of mirrors. Bright red walls pop against a sea of infinity mirrors. The Hôtel de Ville, the city hall of Paris, originally built 1357, expanded in 1533 and reconstructed in 1892, also takes elements from the look.

By the mid-1700s, the rococo style debuted in England through silver decorations made by artisans. Later, St Martin's Lane Academy – known today as the Royal Academy of Arts (RA) – home to the painter and engraver William Hogarth and friends of the book illustrator Hubert-François Gravelot and the painter Andien de Clermont, helped introduce and promote the rococo style in England. The English were famously infatuated with the wonderfully expressive and opulent looks of rococo interiors, and began to imitate them until the furniture designers and cabinet makers Matthias Lock and Henry Copland published a series of prints in 1742 that were distinctive of a new British form of rococo scrollwork. Frequently widely adopted for woodcarving and other decorative work, it remained popular until the mid-1760s.

The Victorian Era

During the Victorian period, maximalism exploded with a focus on details. The Victorian Era is categorized as the 63-year period from 1837–1901, in which Queen Victoria ruled England. There are several reasons why the Victorians took on the maximalist aesthetic in the home during this time, but most likely it is the advent and ease of international travel and the melding of cultures that came with all of that. At the same time, in the United States, the Industrial Revolution was taking place, which allowed newfound sources of income. People would decorate their houses with as many interesting objects as possible, which showed cultural capital and social status.

Victorian maximalism mixes and matches aesthetics from different time periods and various cultures. Think lush velvet curtains, lacquered accessories from Japan, ornate Chinese sculpture and details from the baroque and rococo aesthetics of Italy and France. On a deeper level, the Victorians also wanted to reclaim some of the styles of decorative art that were popular in the past – for example, medieval or gothic. Details such as stained glass, cast iron and marble harked back to some of these very specific interiors.

The Victorians loved beautifully carved wooden furniture and wallpapers, combining prints and ornamentation in their own very unique way. They were some of the first to experiment with all things dramatic, mixing and matching dark colours and patterned walls. Deeper, richer colours, including green and mahogany, were popular and seen on walls and in furniture. Every element of the Victorian home was taken into consideration. For example, walls were painted using various techniques, including sponge painting and marbling, but wallpaper and stencilling were also incredibly popular. One of the most celebrated wallpaper designers was William Morris (1834–96), whose styles epitomized the strong and pure colours of the period and are still much loved today.

Victorian maximalism excelled in the sweeping textiles that took over each room. Take, for example, prints on prints on prints. These were seen on large, comfy sofas, walls and even artwork. The finishing touches in the interiors – such as pillows, lampshades and sconces – were accessorized to the fullest, with gilded features, chunky tassels with resplendent fringes, pleating and unique textures. Tiffany, Christopher Dresser, Christian Herter and Walter Crane were major influences.

opposite *The Linley Sambourne House in London, the home of the* Punch *cartoonist and photographer, retains many of its original Victorian features, such as blue and white Chinese porcelain, Whitefriars glass lampshades and tin-glazed homewares.*

Elsie de Wolfe

Often credited with single-handedly inventing the profession of interior decorating in the United States, Elsie de Wolfe (1865–1950) had her own original style. Also known as Lady Mendl, she was an actress before she started decorating and came from a prominent family. Banishing the darkness and browns from the usual Victorian aesthetic, she approached a new kind of modern maximalism during the era. She once said, 'I believe in plenty of optimism and white paint, comfortable chairs with lights beside them, open fires on the hearth and flowers wherever they "belong", mirrors and sunshine in all rooms.' And to match her flamboyant sense of decorating, she also dressed in a manner that was over the top. Take, for example, the fact that she tinted her hair blue or lavender to match her outfits: 'You will express yourself, in your home, whether you want to or not,' she insisted.

She uniquely positioned herself as someone who valued simplicity, but also regality in the Victorian era. De Wolfe liked bright white and light walls and furniture inspired by the eighteenth-century French rococo style, French antiques, mirrors, white paint, chintz, pastel-coloured furniture and trelliswork motifs on wallpapers. She preferred real painted walls to papered ones and often placed furniture in ways to

encourage conversation. Most important of all, she instilled a sense of much-needed femininity into her work. She would go on to work on many of the pioneering women-centric projects, including the design of the Colony Club, a women-only, private social club in New York City. One of her biggest

projects was the Ladies' Reception Room of the Frick Mansion (now the Boucher Room of the Frick Collection). She received the commission from the American industrialist and arts patron Henry Clay Frick with the specific mention that she did women's rooms better than anyone at the time.

Art Nouveau

Art nouveau took some of the same motifs seen in the Victorian era and emphasized them even more. Think florals, feminine curves, strong silhouettes and linear graphics with a heavy art-world influence. Most of all, the art nouveau period was well-known for dramatic interpretations of nature with super-feminine lines. The designer William Morris, who gained popularity during the Victorian era, helped popularize the look. One of the best examples of the art nouveau interior aesthetic in pop culture is seen in the film *My Fair Lady* (1964), starring Audrey Hepburn and based on George Bernard Shaw's 1913 stage play, *Pygmalion*.

Art nouveau, above all else, was inherently maximalist because it was not just constrained to interiors or architecture. Rather, it ran the gamut across furnishings, jewellery, art and urban design. The Arts and Crafts movement of the UK was a major influence, as was the idea of *Gesamtkunstwerk* ('total work of art') in Germany, which spread through every aspect of visual art and *objets* of the time. The architecture and interior design of Paul Hankar, Henry van de Velde and Victor Horta, whose Hôtel Tassel was completed in 1893 in Brussels, Belgium, were some of the first examples of interior maximalism in art nouveau. The French architect and designer Hector Guimard saw Horta's work in Brussels and was inspired to create the infamous entrances to the new Paris Métro. Louis Tiffany's extreme, almost surreal, curved furniture and bed frames, Alphonse Mucha's famous portraits decorative with curved lines and extreme florals, plus the glassware of René Lalique and Émile Gallé were all hallmarks of the maximal art nouveau period.

'Art nouveau was inspired by all the fluid forms of nature,' Paris-born designer Robert Couturier told *Elle Décor* in March 2019. 'It was a very new thing at the time because most houses were in a heavy Victorian fashion. It also came in a derivative century, where you did not have any style that was really, really new. It was very unexpected and innovative.'

Unlike Victorian maximalism, art nouveau was more all-encompassing and narrowly defined. That's because so much of the design was also about the architecture. For example, lots of grand stained-glass windows, floral elements built into the façades of buildings, as well as plenty of arched ceilings. Art nouveau interiors also did not mix an eclectic genre-defining number of elements together (as the Victorians were so excited to do), but was rather defined by its own look. France's Louis Majorelle was one of the most popular designers who represented the look at the time. The era is also known for its light fixtures by Émile Gallé, which were extremely ornate and maximal.

opposite *Hôtel Tassel in Brussels, Belgium, designed by Victor Horta, displays the soft, feminine lines so distinct to the art nouveau period.*

Florals were everywhere in this style. During the latter half of the Victorian era, japonisme (a French term in reference to the use of Japanese-inspired art) became popular in elements of wall treatments, art and wallpaper, and this became even more established during the art nouveau movement. Hues including muted pink, cream, mint green and bold shades of metallic gold defined the look. Above all else, lines are soft, organic and unexpected: asymmetry was prized and those lines were often categorized as whiplash lines (softly flowing, S-shaped line motifs). Also of importance for the art nouveau era of maximalism was the use of glass, iron and concrete.

left *A 1920s decorated glass table lamp by Émile Gallé.*

left *A Peony table lamp by Tiffany Studios, manufactured with leaded glass and bronze.*

below *The art nouveau bedroom designed by furniture designer Louis Majorelle in Meurthe-et-Moselle, France, famous for its nature-inspired motifs such as stained-glass windows and a bed frame that looks like a butterfly.*

Art Deco

The art deco movement swept up the next era of interiors with a new approach to more is more. Rejecting the ultra-feminine, nature-first aesthetic, it replaced everything with harsh, graphic lines and extreme luxury. Art deco was best associated with the highest luxury and the most advanced technology at the time, such as skyscrapers and luxury ocean liners. But it first appeared in France during the 1910s and was extremely popular in the United States and Europe during the 1920s through the early 1930s. Known for mixing striking geometric lines with rich colours, hard motifs and opulent details, art deco is firmly rooted in a maximalist approach when it comes to interior design. But it didn't stop there: art deco reached jewellery, architecture, art and even everyday product design, from microwaves to vacuum cleaners. Above all else, art deco in interior design represents luxury, opulence and an eye on the future.

Much like its Victorian predecessors, art deco interior maximalism took its references from a variety of different topics, from Cubism and the Vienna Secession to Fauvism, Ballets Russes, Louis XVI and Louis Philippe I. It is also heavily integrated in cross-cultural references, such as the aesthetics of China, Japan, India, Persia (Iran), ancient Egypt and Mayan art.

Art deco was highly connected to interior design – perhaps more so than any other maximalist movement. That's because of the timing. Decorative artists, including interior designers, were long-considered artists without status until the term *arts décoratifs* started being used, giving furniture, textiles and interior decorators official status. In 1868, the *Le Figaro* newspaper used the term *objets d'art décoratifs* to refer to objects used for the stage set created for the Théâtre de l'Opéra. The Société des Artistes Décorateurs (Society of Decorative Artists), or SAD, was founded in 1901 and decorative artists were given the same rights of authorship as painters and sculptors. The movement was heavily rooted in France, too – French designers

above *The art deco bedroom of fashion designer Jeanne Lanvin, designed by Arman-Albert Rateau.*

felt threatened at the time by the increasing exports of cheap German furnishings that were coming to Europe.

The art deco decorators were some of the originals to clash colours and juxtapose highly luxurious objects and materials together in unusual ways. This décor style screamed expensive and was the opposite of quiet luxury. Think exotic materials such as ebony, ivory and silk, contrasted with expensive elements of natural, handmade objects like woven baskets or extravagant

opposite above *The Glass
Salon designed by Paul Ruaud
with furniture by Eileen Gray, for
Juliette Lévy, the milliner of the
boutique J. Suzanne Talbot, Paris,
France, 1922.*

opposite below *A writing
table in green shagreen,
accompanied by a pink satin
upholstered chair, by André
Groult, circa 1925.*

bouquets of flowers. No surface was left behind when it came
to decorative decisions: upholstery, screens, wallpaper, textiles,
carpets and even ceilings were covered in a cacophony of
clashing colours and prints, in bright hues and bold, rich jewel
tones. These over-the-top colours and patterns seen in home
interiors as well as the latest hotels were a direct reflection of
the fashions of the time, such as the work of French fashion
designer Paul Poiret (1879–1944), who focused on bright
hues with cross-cultural references from around the world.
Elsewhere, Cubist and Fauvist painters had an influence on
the maximal colours and luxurious lines and shapes.

Similarly, some of the top fashion designers of the time,
such as Jeanne Lanvin, showed the art deco influence in her
haute-couture work but also lived an art deco lifestyle. Her
Parisian bedroom was designed by Armand-Albert Rateau and
covered with moulded lambris below sculpted bas-reliefs in
stucco. Other elements included marble, sculpted wood and a
cabinet full of decorative objects displayed against a backdrop
of blue silk. And for the bathroom? There was Sienna marble,
chunky bronze fittings and more carved stucco.

Expensive and rare materials that made a bold statement
of more is more were everywhere. Such as when the decorator
Paul Ruaud created the Glass Salon for the Suzanne Talbot
boutique in 1932. It included a floor of matte silvered glass
slabs and an assortment of animal skins, black and white
panelled lacquerwork and a serpentine armchair and two
tubular armchairs by Eileen Gray. Some of the most notable
maximal art-deco interiors were covered in materials that
wowed. Like André Groult's 1925 cabinet covered with
shagreen or sharkskin, or the works of the decorator Émile-
Jacques Ruhlmann, who had a penchant for using mother of
pearl, tortoiseshell and ivory as inlays and also used rosewood,
ebony and silk in his designs wherever he could. Furniture
designers Louis Süe and André Mare (Atelier Français) became
infamous as a French interior design firm using super-
expensive materials to decorate transatlantic ocean liners.

English Eccentricity

The English have long-prized maximalist tradition in interiors. Think unexpected prints, clashing art and colours the rest of Europe wouldn't dare to use. They were some of the first to take Paisley, which has its roots in Iran, and use it in Europe in the 1800s. By the early twentieth century, they were mixing in new references to the interior scene, pulling from Raj-era India with heavily embellished furniture, hot pinks, glaring saffrons and more. Some of the popular designers, eccentrics and influential leaders at the time were looking at references from baroque Italy, Gothic Revival, Napoleon III style in France, as well as the Oriental influence, blending them all together in ways no one else was. On a more extreme (and colourful) level, it was a complex take on what the Victorians had started doing.

In 1933, Sibyl Colefax (1874–1950) founded her interior design business, known today as Colefax and Fowler. She would go on to have one of the most iconic influences on quirky English design. In 1938, she partnered with highly regarded decorator John Fowler (1906–77). Colefax was known for covering the walls in a barrage of art, highly dramatic lighting and mismatched pairings of furniture from Europe mixed with chinoiserie elements. Later on, the famous twentieth-century tastemaker and interior designer Nancy Lancaster (1897–1994), alongside John Fowler, would invent the look of the eccentric English country house. Her famous rule to live by was to always add 'something a little bit ugly' to every room and she described her work as a decorator as 'a bit like mixing a salad'.

In the early 1900s, the explosion of artists, thinkers and writers known as the Bloomsbury Group had a major influence on interiors at Charleston in East Sussex. Serving as the modernist home of the English painter and interior designer Vanessa Bell (1879–1961), sister of the writer Virginia Woolf, the brick farmhouse was rented by her and fellow artist Duncan Grant in 1916. Inspired to live without the conventional ideals of Edwardian society, the duo took influences from Italian frescos and the post-impressionists, treating their home interiors like a living work of art, hand-painting every single surface with portraits, motifs, florals and other patterns, then covering the walls with even more art. Today, the East Sussex space is a museum. It's the perfect example of art and interiors colliding and their everlasting influence, with the murals, painted furniture, textiles, paintings and ceramics in the interior, all extremely representative of the Bloomsbury Group.

opposite above *Colefax and Fowler's country-style furnishings decorate a 1990s interior.*

opposite below *A view of the modernist home and studio of painters Vanessa Bell and Duncan Grant at Charleston in East Sussex.*

Dorothy Draper

Often considered one of the most influential interior designers of all time, Dorothy Draper (1889–1969) was a key player in the maximalist movement. She came from an extremely wealthy and privileged background, allowing her to have incredible connections and freedom to interpret historical interior design. Nonetheless, she built the pathway for many maximalist interior designers to come. Consider the fact that she revolutionized the industry with a new kind of look that took inspiration from baroque. She was also revolutionary for the fact that she was one of the first interior design companies in the United States. Founded in 1923 and dubbed Dorothy Draper and Company, the business was unheard of at the time, especially for a woman.

Draper broke away from the typical 'period room' styles previously seen in contemporary interior design of the past, honing in on her own version of baroque, which she called 'modern baroque'. Her emphasis was on bold colour, which felt especially new, yet she took classical elements from the baroque period, creating elaborate plasterwork and ornate, gilded details. All things vibrant came together with splashy pinks, deep purples, yellow-greens, bold blues and one of her signature looks: white with a very particular pairing of shiny, lacquered black. She loved black and white stripes and chequered floors, and frequently utilized them throughout her work. Together with chintz prints, panelled, lacquered doors and opulent mirror frames, she created vignettes of drama through wide-open spaces that wowed.

Draper deeply appeals to the anti-minimal aesthetic. Her first big break was in the early 1930s when Douglas Elliman commissioned her to re-do the Carlyle Hotel on Madison Avenue, Manhattan. She designed the extremely glamorous

opposite *A nod to rococo at the Draper-designed Quitandinha Palace in Rio de Janeiro, Brazil.*

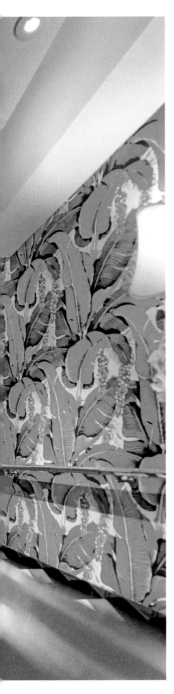

Greenbrier hotel (the Victorian writing room was once described as the most photographed room in the United States), in White Sulphur Springs, West Virginia, as well as the Quitandinha Palace and Casino Resort in Petrópolis, Brazil, the Arrowhead Springs Hotel in California and Hampshire House in New York.

Even though Draper's decadent work was seen in some of America's most luxurious hotels and resorts (and the homes of the ultra-wealthy and celebrities), her maximal influence touched the lives of many through her other work. Consider the fact that she famously advised people to 'take that red and paint your front door with it' during the Great Depression in her 'Ask Dorothy Draper' column, which ran in 70 newspapers. She also had her own line of over-the-top fabrics and sold over a million yards of her signature cabbage rose chintz.

left *A stairway at the Greenbrier hotel in West Virginia showcases Dorothy Draper's banana leaf wallpaper.*

above *A Draper upholstered chair and carpet in an orchid design inside the presidential suite of the Greenbriar.*

Hollywood Regency

Inspired by the glamorous and opulent era of Hollywood stars, Hollywood Regency was born in the 1930s with the idea in mind of taking highly lavish elements of gold, bronze and mirrored details, and combining them with wooden mid-century furniture. Interior designer Dorothy Draper made the style well known in the 1930s through the 1950s. But the look remains popular today, with some of the most celebrated decorators, such as Kelly Wearstler, using elements of it in their work. Many contemporary homes draw from the Hollywood Regency style of interior design, especially when it comes to specific features such as mirrors, bar trolleys and artwork.

This look is all about over-the-top glitz and glamour, and was modelled after Hollywood's Golden Age from the 1920s through the 1960s. Designer Charles William 'Billy' Haines (1900–73) also played a prominent role in creating masterpieces that utilized this aesthetic. With inspiration from parts of rococo and art deco, Hollywood Regency takes the lavish, opulent side of design and reinterprets it through a new era of design that feels at home alongside the Hollywood productions that took place during the mid-century period. There's an emphasis on brighter colours such as pinks, turquoise and yellows. Prints were streamlined: think chequerboard patterns. And large mirrors, windows and decadent displays were everywhere. Mirrored details appeared on everything from dressers to trays and even entire walls, echoing the total embodiment of glamour.

opposite *Hollywood elegance in the Billy Haines-designed Holmby Hills, California, home of Betsy Bloomingdale, circa 1960s. The house was subsequently sold to fashion designer Tom Ford.*

Unlike a lot of other maximalist design genres of the past, Hollywood Regency attempted to put a focus on comfort and familiarity. Like the American country-style interior genre that emerged around the same time, overstuffed, tufted sofas in large floral prints reigned supreme. In place of leather chairs in the Chesterfield style or simple rocking chairs, Hollywood Regency-era seating was larger than life in shape, silhouette and print. Think of damask slipcovered wing chairs, black and white motifs and animal prints, such as leopard or zebra, that bring together the sense of luxury and opulent glamour seen in the movies. While bright, golden details previously appeared in art nouveau and rococo through floral and nature-inspired pieces, Hollywood Regency reclaimed the look via a different kind of vision, featuring sunbursts, hearts and bamboo.

The thing to really keep in mind about Hollywood Regency is that it's totally unapologetic in its maximalist approach to glamour. It's never too much since it's based on the Golden Age of Hollywood cinema, where everything was opulent and optimistically overdone. Even the furnishings in Hollywood Regency shined bright – often done in lacquered surfaces that were mirror-like and glossy in appearance, they popped against a sea of brass and black and white. Velvet and silks sang through textiles and in upholstery, meanwhile, fur was a fixture in rugs and on pillows. Lucite was another popular choice for items such as golden detailed vanities and chairs, both of which sparkled in the maximalist interior. Porcelain objects, pop art and animal statues have added a hint of humour and kitsch to the Hollywood Regency style over time.

left *Draper's interior for the Greenbrier hotel showcases the Hollywood Regency features of glass and crystal accents against a bold colour palette. Often called the 'mother of modern baroque', the designer used decorative elements of contrasting baby pink and scarlet red.*

Sister Parish

Wealthy socialite-turned-decorator Sister Parish (1910–94) brought a new kind of maximalism to the American interiors scene. The New Yorker was the first practitioner brought in to decorate the Kennedy White House. Based in New York City, the Great Depression forced Parish to take on work and in 1933, the 23-year-old opened a decorating business. She was completely untrained, but her first cousin was the acclaimed interior decorator Dorothy Draper.

Very quickly, she began defining a new kind of look: one that took the classic elements of the American farmhouse and made it more exaggerated, colourful and filled with prints. Previously, the Farmhouse style valued simplicity. After living in New York City, Parish moved to a farmhouse on Long Lane in Far Hills, New Jersey, which she decorated herself. It was here that she really honed her own personal style, intentionally mismatching prints and patterns, placing various items off-centre, painting wood furniture white and experimenting with brightly painted floors. She loved integrating American arts and crafts into her work, such as needlepoint and quilts, and would go on to inspire American icons including the fashion designer Ralph Lauren and the entertaining icon Martha Stewart. And her clients? Among the elite coterie were Brooke Astor, Ann Getty, Oscar de la Renta, Rachel Lambert 'Bunny' Mellon, Jane Engelhard, Enid Haupt and William Paley.

'Her interiors as a rule were refreshingly unstudied, unself-conscious, and unstrained,' according to a 1999 *Architectural Digest* article describing Parish's style. 'A Sister Parish room overflowed, to be sure – but buoyantly. It was romantic and whimsical but not sentimental; and, always, it was light – the rug might be Aubusson, the mirror Chippendale and the chandelier Waterford, but she undercut these "brand names" with all manner of charming distractions. Her living rooms lived: They were friendly to the world...'

above *Sister Parish's home in Dark Harbor, Maine. Her best work included contrasting prints and plenty of florals.*

Tony Duquette

King of excess, Los Angeles native Tony Duquette (1914–99) was among those to make the most impact on the maximalist movement. He began making a big splash in the 1940s and worked up until the 1980s. His great-uncle was Peter Paul Marshall, the business partner of the Pre-Raphaelite artist and designer William Morris. Duquette's work was prolifically over the top and perhaps most notable of all was his penchant for using very affordable (often considered cheap) materials to create a sense of grandeur. Take, for example, his Hollywood Hills studio, which included a mix of eighteenth-century French antiques, golden trees and a ceiling studded with plastic serving trays that were glued on. Like Duquette himself, his clients (Vincente Minnelli, Doris Duke, Mary Pickford, J. Paul Getty, David O. Selznick and the Duchess of Windsor) appreciated an overdone sense of grandeur that took bits and bobs from baroque, rococo, art deco and Hollywood Regency, but with his own very personal twist: Duquette was always all about fantasy.

Duquette often said that he was discovered by Lady Mendl (the interior decorator known as Elsie de Wolfe). The two collaborated until her death in 1951. Throughout the 1940s, Duquette's maximalist aesthetic was key to his many projects, from furnishing a castle for Elizabeth Arden to designing his first piece of jewellery for the Duchess of Windsor. Also key to his aesthetic was a sort of collage-like creative process, of sourcing odds and ends from various unexpected places and bringing them together, just as he did for his own 175-acre Malibu ranch home, named Sortilegium. It featured Oriental and Georgian motifs, a window from Greta Garbo and John Gilbert's house, a Venetian gondola and a set of eighteenth-century doors presented to him and his wife by Mary Pickford and Buddy Rogers as a wedding present. Duquette's flair for the dramatic was recognized and he also designed for debutante balls and opera sets. 'Decorating is not a surface performance,' he once said. 'It's a spiritual impulse, inborn and primordial.' Above all else, it was about celebrating the individual and putting a ban on all things boring and beige.

opposite *Tony Duquette's Dawnridge, located in Beverly Hills, California, encompasses opulence and excess in the form of antiques and colourful masterpieces created by the designer himself.*

overleaf left *Rich colours and dynamic textures dominate the tent room in Duquette's West Hollywood, California, Outpost residence.*

overleaf right *The living room in Duquette's Outpost was full of jewel-toned colours such as sapphire, ruby and topaz.*

Billy Baldwin

Placing colour and personality at the forefront of his work, designer Billy Baldwin (1903–83) made a major impact with his work. He began his career in 1935, working with Ruby Ross Wood, eventually taking over the firm when she passed away in 1950. In 1952, he formed his own firm, Baldwin and Martin, with Edward Martin. He may be best known for the vibrant, all-red living room that he created for the legendary fashion editor, Diana Vreeland: 'Red is the great clarifier – bright, cleansing, revealing. It makes all colours beautiful. I can't imagine being bored with it. It would be like becoming tired of the person you love,' she declared. And so, Vreeland told the Park Avenue interior designer that she wanted her living room to 'look like a garden, but a garden in hell'. To Baldwin, mixing comfort with upscale luxury was key. He adored pure cotton and loathed silk, and more than anything, was a fan of having books – lots of them – in interior spaces.

Baldwin often layered different materials and various prints and patterns together when working and the same was true of his approach to Vreeland's apartment. Here, he added mirrored walls, crystal sconces, old fashion busts, crocheted afghan blankets and decorative shells. 'I knew what that meant: red,' he wrote in his 1974 memoir, *Billy Baldwin Remembers*. The infamous red fabric Baldwin used for Vreeland was a bright red scarlet chintz topped with Persian flowers from the London decorator John Fowler: 'I raced home with yards and yards of it,' he wrote, 'and we covered the whole room – walls, curtains, furniture, the works.' Add to that ample supplies of English armchairs, needlepoint pillows and sumptuous amounts of richly luxurious fabrics. Truly maximalist in its appeal, no surface was left uncovered.

'I know that you know me well enough to know that I adore things. I realize that you have hardly enough room to put your cigarette in an ashtray because there's hardly any room to put an ashtray on the table. Another vase of flowers on the table doesn't bother me if the flowers are divine,' the designer recalls Diana Vreeland stating in *Billy Baldwin: An Autobiography* (1985).

Vreeland was far from being this maximalist designer's only client, however. In fact, he worked with a celebrated clientele: Jackie Onassis, Pamela Harriman, Nan Kempner, Bunny Mellon, Babe Paley and many more. His style was distinctly American but also influenced by French furniture and the bold, vivid and bright colours of the French visualist Henri Matisse's paintings. He strongly believed that decorating was a collaborative project and that it was imperative to include furnishings already belonging to the client in the space, so that personal style came above all else.

Baldwin started many of the maximalist trends that live on today. Take, for example, the way that he completely covered the walls of Cole Porter's Waldorf Astoria suite in

tortoiseshell vinyl and designed and built floor-to-ceiling brass étagères instead of using the typical built-in bookcases that were popular at the time. A few years later, those étagères were seen everywhere. Similarly, he decorated William and Babe Paley's New York City apartment inside the St Regis Hotel with a beautiful and unique shirred geometric fabric. A multi-talented character, he published several books about his work and life, and also designed his own line of furniture (including his famous Slipper chair).

'When you are decorating, you must learn to break some rules, but not all of them,' he declared. 'Take the case of pattern on pattern. Some decorators today think you can mix prints. Not so. That just results in confusion.' He also stated, 'It is very important when mixing furnishings of different provenance that there be some kind of connection, so that they can be good neighbours, such as placing a superb modern table next to an antique chair. It would look all wrong. There wouldn't be any connection of quality.'

above *Diana Vreeland's all-red apartment, designed by Billy Baldwin.*

The Swinging Sixties

The heavily striped and patterned carpets of the Swinging Sixties owe much to the designer David Hicks (1929–98). His small-scale hexagonal designs that seemed to float and elevate the room were his signature look and he quickly became one of the icons of maximalist design during the 1960s and 1970s. Many of his pieces have gone on to become collector's items. In fact, Hicks' Hexagon geometric repeat featured prominently in Stanley Kubrick's 1980 psychological horror film, *The Shining*. His work included projects for Windsor Castle, the Prince of Wales and Buckingham Palace, Vidal Sassoon, Helena Rubinstein and the Condé Nast family, among others.

A man of many talents ranging far beyond colour and print, Hicks also worked as a photographer, painter and sculptor, producing fashion and jewellery collections. He wrote nine design books too. Famously English, he was considered a rebellious spirit for breaking away from the more conventional English interiors style, instead using unexpected colour combinations, antiques and highly graphic, original geometric prints. For example, he loathed chintz and, for Helena Rubinstein, created a living room with purple tweed walls and Victorian furniture, upholstered in magenta leather. He also designed sets for the 1968 film *Petulia*, starring Julie Christie and George C. Scott. Hicks would go on to have a major impact on design, in London and beyond.

'My greatest contribution as an interior designer has been to show people how to use bold colour mixtures, how to use patterned carpets, how to light rooms and how to mix old with new,' he wrote in *David Hicks on Living – with Taste* (1968).

Elsewhere, the dress shops in London naturally had a huge influence on what were considered fashionable interiors of the

right *Biba, the 1970s London boutique, incorporated different eras of maximalism and melded them together in a visual fantasy.*

opposite *David Hicks was known for framing his rooms with borders, as seen here in this bold orange room in Lord and Lady Cholmondeley's Hyde Park apartment, London, circa 1965.*

left *Hicks in a maximalist patterned monochrome interior.*

day. The daughter of a Polish diplomat, Barbara Hulanicki opened her iconic fashion boutique Biba in a former chemist's shop in London's Abingdon Road. Covered in chequerboard floors with decadent art nouveau chandeliers, the interior of the ultra-popular youth culture boutique mirrored the fashions. Biba was inspired by bygone eras (particularly Pre-Raphaelite and art nouveau) and decorated in rich, deep colours such as olive green and bruised purple. Hulanicki sought to transform the retail interior into something that felt experiential

and social, filling her shop with ornate Victorian furniture and antiques.

Similarly, on the cusp of the Swinging Sixties, Virginia Bates, a former actress who appeared in the BBC series *Doctor Who* and the film *A Clockwork Orange* (1971), opened her shop in London. Vibrant stained-glass lamps, grand Victorian furniture, mirrors meshed with cabinets full of silver jewellery, dazzling clutches and diamond-adorned headpieces from the 1930s and 1940s created their own maximalist interior. Bates was clearly a purveyor of antiques, not merely vintage.

Mario Buatta

Dubbed both the Prince of Chintz and the Master of More, Mario Buatta (1935–2018) was an Italian-American interior designer who had a keen sense of piling on the prints. Lime green, baby blue, pastel pink and pastel lemon ... Buatta approached colour with a sense of joy. He took the traditional style of the English country home and turned it on its head, with an overdone kaleidoscope of colour, texture and furniture, while still keeping in mind the basic functions and settings of the English country home. Most of all, he was inspired by what he called 'historical clutter', which typically amounts to heirloom objects passed down through generations and seen in this setting.

Mario Buatta started his own business in 1963 after working in the decorating departments of stores such as B. Altman and Company and for the interior designer Dorothy Draper. In the early 1960s, he worked for Keith Irvine, a well-known decorator, for less than a year. He later met the English designer John Fowler, who greatly influenced him as a mentor.

His clients ranged from the super-rich to the super-infamous, including Mariah Carey, Nelson Doubleday, Charlotte Ford, Billy Joel, Peter Duchin and Malcolm Forbes. Many credit his international fame to his 1988 work on Blair House, the official guesthouse for distinguished foreign dignitaries in Washington, with the interior designer, Mark Hampton.

Buatta spent years working on some of his rooms. Most of all, he was a maximalist, but a luxurious one at that. He was given the moniker the Prince of Chintz for his fondness of the cotton fabric with a glazed finish and he used it on everything. According to *The New York Times* in 2018, some of his tassels cost 'hundreds of dollars each and fabrics hundreds of dollars a yard; curtains in a Buatta room might cost $12,000 in today's money by the time they were hung. And painting a Buatta room, which could involve six or seven coats on a

above *A Mario Buatta interior in a New York apartment, with aubergine glazed walls and custom seating by De Angelis in a quadrille print.*

canvas wall covering, plus stippling or staining and finally glazing, could easily come to the equivalent of $23,000 today.'

Though a noted Staten Island, New York-born and bred personality, Mario

Buatta has often been described as Anglophile. He was highly influenced by English interior design, especially from the Regency period, and was also an avid collector of antiques.

Vincent Fourcade

Known for his lavishly, opulent aesthetic that brought a new kind of Victorian and rococo influence to design in the 1980s, Vincent Fourcade (1934–92) was the ultimate French designer in New York, who loved over-the-top European design. He used piles of brocades, velvets, tassels, fringe and genuine French furniture in all of his creations. His style screamed expensive and he wasn't shy about it, often aligning himself with an aristocratic lifestyle. Think fur bed throws, Napoleon III carpets, fringed silk lampshades, deeply coloured velvets … and always a dash of red.

Working with his partner, Robert Denning, the duo created interiors that represented a new kind of high luxury. Dubbed Style Rothschild, their look was often imitated around the world. The apartment decorated for the film adaptation of Tom Wolfe's 1987 novel, *The Bonfire of the Vanities*, was modelled after a Denning and Fourcade design. Clients ranged from Hélène and Michel David-Weill to the Italian politician and Fiat heiress Susanna Agnelli and the legendary fashion designer, Oscar de la Renta.

One of their first – and most elaborate – designs came courtesy of decorating the Seventh Regiment Armory in New York for a benefit to support cancer care. Instead of working with ribbons or bows, they covered the floors with wall-to-wall raccoon, made from 100 old coats, and lined the walls with Fortuny fabrics. They proudly displayed French furniture, with sofas arranged back-to-back – a signature of theirs. 'Outrageous luxury is what our clients want. We have taught them to prefer excess,' Fourcade declared. Like many of the interior designers of his generation, Fourcade was not trained formally in the trade: 'I learned my trade by going out every evening as a young man,' he told the art historian Rosamond Bernier. 'I went to every pretty house in France and Italy and other places, too, and I remembered them all, even down to what was on each little table.'

opposite *Vincent Fourcade in his New York apartment. His desk was made of Coromandel lacquer screens; beneath is a K'ang Hsi temple jar.*

Postmodernism

Kitsch became king and maximalism pushed the boundaries further under the postmodernist movement, which began as early as the 1940s, but reached mainstream popularity in the 1960s. The style had massive influence until the 1990s. But to understand maximal postmodernist interior design, one has to understand postmodern architecture. It was in direct response to the modernist movement that was happening at the time, which prioritized minimalism and simplicity. In the face of modernism, postmodernism flew fast in the other direction, playing with colour, pattern and even humour and whimsy.

When thinking about postmodernist maximalism, many frequently cite the architect Robert Venturi (1925–2018). Similarly, the architect Ludwig Mies van der Rohe (1886–1969) famously said, 'Less is more,' to which Venturi responded, 'Less is a bore.' In postmodernist design, ornamentation, over-the-top exaggerations and wide-ranging cultural references are everything.

The postmodernist interiors repurposed graphic shapes and lines and made them oversized and colourful. They clashed pattern and print and added over-the-top elements that could be considered garish; it was a look that was whimsically curious. Take, for example, the large palm trees seen in the Robert A. M. Stern's residence and pool house in Llewellyn Park, New Jersey, 1982.

In postmodernist maximal interior design, all kinds of prints and patterns are put together in contrasting ways. Historical and traditional elements of interior design are posed in new ways of thinking. For example, Roman-style columns might be covered in chequerboard prints and a fireplace could be painted cobalt blue. Nothing is too kitsch: giant elephants, purple owl statues, wooden palm tree cut-outs in shades of oceanic blue. In John Outram's Duncan Hall at Rice University located in Houston, Texas, 1996, for

opposite *The interior of the University of Cambridge's Judge Business School, at the old Addenbrooke's Hospital in Cambridge, designed by John Outram and completed in 1995.*

above *The Chippendale chair designed by Venturi from 1978–83, made of laminated wood and plastic laminate, inspired 1980s patterns and motifs.*

opposite *A 1981 re-edition of Alessandro Mendini's 1978 Proust chair, made of hand-painted wood and upholstery.*

example, the British architect left no surface (even the ceiling) bare, covering everything in tons of colourful graphic lines and clashing prints. Postmodernist interiors were often fun, contradictory and with an element of childlike wonder and surrealism: form does not follow function.

One of the most influential designers of the maximal postmodernist era was Alessandro Mendini (1931–2019), who not only worked in the industry as a designer and architect, but also brought attention to this kind of radical design through his work with Italian design magazines including *Casabella*, *Modo* and *Domus*. Mendini valued bold prints, bright colours and designs that made the viewer or user question everything. Take, for example, one of his most infamous projects, the 1978 Proust armchair. The once decadently carved, wood-frame baroque armchair with white upholstery was turned on its head as Mendini projected a slide onto it and hand-painted a pointillism pattern. Since then, it's been redesigned again and again with different extreme prints and seen throughout decades of postmodernist interiors.

Memphis Group

Growing out of the postmodernist interior design design movement came Memphis. This Italian-led maximalist aesthetic was a favourite of celebrities such as the musician superstar David Bowie and fashion designer Karl Lagerfeld in the 1980s and 1990s, but continues to have a huge influence on the way we look at and decorate maximal interiors today.

Take, for instance, Ettore Sottsass's Ultrafragola mirror, which is a plastic, pink light-up mirror rendered with wavy lines epitomizing femininity. Today, it's impossible not to see the Ultrafragola in maximalist interiors on social media and they are all over the homes of celebrities such as Lena Dunham and Bella Hadid. The mirror first debuted at Milan's Eurodomus 3 trade show in 1970, in which Florentine manufacturer Poltronova unveiled Mobili Grigi, an eclectic bedroom set designed by Sottsass. The entire collection was made of sleek, vacuum-moulded plastic and cast fibreglass. Overall, it represented the new movement of artistic interior maximalism – to bring novel appeal to formerly harsh, industrial materials frequently seen in the home. For the most part, the designs in this collection were sparsely produced, except for the Ultrafragola, which means 'the ultimate strawberry' in Italian.

All this is to say that the Ultrafragola was part of a much wider movement that shaped maximalist interiors: Memphis. In 1981, a group of designers in Milan took postmodernism to the next level of grandeur. Memphis was founded by Ettore Sottsass, but the distinguished group also included Nathalie du Pasquier, Peter Shire, Michael Graves, George Sowden, Michele De Lucchi and others. They continued the clashing colours, intentionally glaring shapes and mixed patterns and emphasis on wacky geometric forms that the postmodernists started out, but took it to a new level of kitsch that was even bright and bolder, like a cartoon brought to life throughout the 1980s and 1990s.

Everything about Memphis interiors revolves around the look and the element of reinterpreting the everyday into something new and (sometimes) non-functional – for example, a bookshelf with graphic, non-functioning shelves or clashing, zig-zagging prints in primary colours.

Once upon a time, the inimitable Chanel and Chloé designer Karl Lagerfeld lived in an apartment in Monaco that was entirely decorated in Memphis décor (see pages 86–7). It was the early 1980s and Lagerfeld was just beginning to get into his prime with his early Chanel collections. A unique aesthetic was something that was obvious, something that he, a collector through and through, decided to take beyond fashion and

opposite *A Marilyn Monroe portrait by Andy Warhol is reflected in the much-imitated Ultrafragola mirror by Ettore Sottsass.*

traverse into a total lifestyle too. Even as an infamous collector, Lagerfeld would often give away his personal belongings as lavish gifts or sell them on. The Karl Lagerfeld Memphis design period would unfortunately come to a close when Sotheby's held an auction of Lagerfeld's Memphis collection in 1991.

Maximal Memphis looks are not for the faint of heart. They are highly specific and very geometric. Unlike other maximalist interior movements, Memphis feels less referential to other time periods and cultures. And perhaps that is what made it so specific and, in many ways, so short-lived. After all, the Memphis design group was only active from 1981 to 1988, though Sottsass's mirrors and other collectible icons live on.

opposite *The Carlton Room Divider, 1981, by Ettore Sottsass.*

above *Nathalie du Pasquier's interior design sketch* Room with Radio *from 1984.*

Kawaii Culture

Born in 1970 in Japan, Sebastian Masuda is known as the pioneer of the kawaii aesthetic, often referred to as the King of Kawaii or the Father of Kawaii. Working as an artist in the world of theatre, he eventually opened up 6%DokiDoki in Ura-Harajuku, Tokyo, in 1995. The shop sells fashion, clothing and accessories worn by everyone from members of group Blackpink to rapper Nicki Minaj.

Kawaii is roughly described as the 'culture of cuteness' and Masuda brings that vision to interiors. Most influential is his work in Tokyo and New York. He created and designed the Kawaii Monster Café in Harajuku, which attracted a huge number of tourists as well as stars such as Kim Kardashian and Dua Lipa, to name but a few. Open from 2015 to 2021, the café was one of the best examples of kawaii-culture interiors. Dream-like, giant colourful mushrooms hung over the vibrant seating, while three-dimensional figures of rabbits and sheep hung from the ceiling, eyes glowing. The animals on the merry-go-round were surreal, as if they had been dunked in cake frosting and doused in shiny beads. With a disco ball ceiling and swirls of colour everywhere you looked, there was nothing else quite like it.

In 2023, Masuda opened up his first restaurant in New York City, Sushidelic, which has a kawaii-adorned conveyor belt full of glittering cats, bows and other decorative objects.

below *A kaleidoscope of wacky colour in Sebastian Musada's girl's room installation at the Salone del Mobile, Milan, Italy.*

opposite *The Kawaii Monster Café in Tokyo, Japan, was a pinnacle of kawaii interior design.*

Contemporary Maximalism

Today, modern maximalism draws on references from all over and celebrates some of the most important maximalist eras of the past, from Victorian to Hollywood Regency. Current maximalism is about more is more and doesn't focus on one particular genre but rather, embraces everything and is entirely dominated by personal preference as much as style. It's about a refined mix of prints, patterns, objects and displays that come together to form a highly curated mix.

Perhaps rather unexpectedly, contemporary maximalism represents every kind of maximalism we've witnessed in the past, with a new point of view. Take, for example, the idea of 'cluttercore', which has recently emerged. For many, this is a style that feels nostalgic because, in some ways, it recalls the bedrooms of teenage girls, with various pieces of jewellery hanging from racks, stacks of books and magazines, plastered cut-outs and posters on the walls and lots of little tchotchkes (small decorative objects) scattered throughout. In some ways, it feels like a reaction to the minimalist aesthetic and cookie-cutter homes and interiors spawned by Instagram and influencer culture. Cluttercore is personal: it's lived-in, and not easily replicable from person to person. There's a line between collecting and just having lots of stuff and being messy, and this strikes the right balance. If you love your stuff, why not display it?

In today's landscape, historically maximalist homes are still regarded as highly influential. Take Ann and Gordon Getty's iconic 1913 home in San Francisco's Pacific Heights neighbourhood, for example. Bringing together museum-worthy European antiques, Chinese sculptures, Venetian paintings, French textiles and Russian chandeliers, the space is an incredible example of interior decorator Ann's aesthetic and

right *Interior designer Ann Getty, wife of oil tycoon Gordon Getty, at her lavishly decorated maximalist home in San Francisco.*

influence. Similarly, in contemporary maximalism, there's a new generation of designers that are shaking things up and doing things differently. Entire brands exist that are catered to the maximalist interior lover – House of Hackney, for example. This English brand specializes in dramatic prints, offering matching sofas, curtains, pillows and every other home product one could think of.

One of the most maximalist of contemporary maximalist designers is interior architect Martin Brudnizki, known for taking a theme and pushing it to its limits. One of his most famous projects of all was the 2018 revamp of Annabel's, the kitsch London private club. Done in an ornate fashion with a flowered bathroom ceiling, palm tree columns and more, more, more mirrors and trelliswork, it has become one of the most-Instagrammable club

interiors of all time. The Stockholm-born designer founded Martin Brudnizki Design Studio in London before opening a New York studio in 2012. He now works with over 80 interior designers, architects, lighting designers, product designers and art consultants together in his studio.

In 2022, Brudnizki took his predilection for themes even further with the Bacchanalia restaurant in Mayfair, London. The space is covered in classical Greek and Roman mythology-inspired imagery, including statues by the controversial artist Damien Hirst. The designer goes all out for projects like these, enlisting some of the most talented

opposite *The terrace at Annabel's club in London features textiles by House of Hackney.*

below *The Elephant Bar at Annabel's designed by Martin Brudnizki.*

people to work alongside him. Like the artist Gary Myatt, who painted floor-to-ceiling murals inspired by interpretations of the French artist Thomas Couture's 1847 painting, *The Romans in their Decadence*. Look closely at his work to find minor but major details, such as how the flowers at Annabel's are actually fake, or how the people in the paintings at Bacchanalia are actually using iPhones and laptops despite their historical depiction. Myatt has also worked on Four Seasons Hotels and Resorts, The Beekman, Cecconi's and more.

Similarly, positioned as one of the modern masters of maximalist design, Ken Fulk has designed homes, restaurants and hotels as well as working to create experiential weddings, parties and family getaways. If ever there was a designer who was inspired by being the life and soul of the party and living for the party, it would be him, as he layers on print, colour and more print over and over and over again. It's no wonder Pharrell Williams and Gigi Hadid are among his clients.

Establishing herself as one of the most prominent interior maximalists, Kelly Behun has also made a name for herself with her artful juxtapositions. She often takes contrasting, mismatched items and pairs them in quirky ways: 'An igloo meets a yurt but with a Bugatti chair, it's all good to me,' she told *Cultured* magazine in 2022. 'I love the variety. It's all about figuring out what excites the client. It's also important to have a bit of irreverence and not take things too seriously. I learned this from working with Philippe Starck.'

Behun often works on some of the most exciting hotel designs, including Miami Beach's Delano and the Mondrian in Los Angeles, but that doesn't stop her from adding highly personal touches, like fine art from some of the most exciting emerging artists, to her spaces. In the past, her work has displayed hand-painted chairs by the California artist Kim MacConnel, textile artist Mitsuko Asakura, ceramics collections by MyungJin Kim, Makoto Kagoshima, Takuro Kuwata, Roger Herman, Jeremy Anderson, Shizue Imai, Adrienne Fierman and Monty J.

'We try to be thoughtful about how we bring these elements into the home,' Behun told *Cultured*. 'I don't profess to be an art advisor, but I like to be a connector and point clients in the right direction when it comes to galleries in New York and elsewhere. I like to highlight the talents I'm excited about and that are worth following.'

Keeping up the tradition of English eccentricity in interiors, designers such as Luke Edward Hall are embodying the maximalist spirit of mixing and matching oddball combinations together to create striking displays of Englishness. Take, for example, his work for the Hôtel Les Deux Gares in Paris, which includes all kinds of stripes and geometric lines and shapes smashed and mashed together. The rising design star is new to the scene, but nonetheless, making an impact internationally: 'I do think that humour is important. I don't mean in a laugh-out-loud kind of way, but I like things – furniture,

above *A Kelly Behun-designed room with a Kinder modern rug, wallpaper by Studio Printworks and a sunburst mirror by Misha Kahn.*

left *An interior design by Luke Edward Hall and Duncan Campbell with a backdrop of botanical wallpaper by Svenskt Tenn Josef Frank.*

below *The Kelly Wearstler-designed Proper hotel in downtown Los Angeles.*

fabrics, colours – that put a smile on a face, or raise an eyebrow,' he told *Vogue Australia* in 2022. 'I like a bit of camp, a bit of wit. I'm not really into serious, sober interiors. There is a time and a place for them, but I'd get bored and sad in a neutral box.'

Many of the contemporary maximalist designers of today focus on and prioritize endless amounts of colour and print. Take, for example, Studio Sam Buckley. Combining unexpected hues, shapes and textures, Buckley decorates spaces but also creates bespoke pieces, from fine cabinetry and case goods to hand-knotted carpets and furniture designs. Filling every space to the brim, he takes a 360-degree approach to maximalism through covering the walls, floors and even the ceilings of his spaces.

Other maximalist contemporary designers are making their name for infusing over-the-top signatures with a glammed-up vintage aesthetic. That's the case for Kelly Wearstler, who has always been inspired by her mother's career in the antiques industry. Since her early teens, Wearstler has been collecting vintage clothing, which also has its own influence on her work. In particular, she weaves in the look and feel of some of the madcap maximalist aesthetics of the past, from art deco to Hollywood Regency. In fact, it's almost impossible to view her work without seeing some element of Hollywood Regency, whether it is in one of the mirrors or one of the heavy, bronze lighting fixtures. Above all else, she makes the case for modern maximalism with a hint of old and new. She also has created her

own aesthetic, one that takes heavily from the flavours and tastes of California and Los Angeles, where she is based.

The New York Times called Wearstler the Mother of 'Eclectic' Interior Design and rightly so. She rose to prominence in the early 2000s, has written multiple books and worked with everyone from the singer Gwen Stefani to designing the restaurant at Bergdorf Goodman and the Proper hotel in downtown Los Angeles. Wearstler layers things together that don't conventionally match, oftentimes opting for furniture and other accessories that are the opposite of minimalist. They are weighty, heavy, large and imposing.

'I'm constantly moving forward and pushing myself – I don't want to repeat myself. As a designer, I'm a free spirit. It's like a moving target,' she told *The New York Times* in 2023 when asked to describe her style. With millions of followers on Instagram, she is a celebrity in her own right. She is also a favourite of the fashion world and can often be seen wearing high-fashion outfits featuring current season designer pieces from Margiela, Loewe, Alaïa and Prada, gravitating towards big boxy power blazers and baggy jeans with a statement shoe and bag.

Likewise, Justina Blakeney is another designer who is maximally led with a celebrity-like following. She is an American designer, artist, interior designer, writer and speaker who plays with maximal style with an epic sense of bohemian. Think beautifully tiled floors and bright furnishings styled alongside elements such as woven rope, fur throws, tassels and lots and lots and lots of big, green plants. She founded a homeware and home decoration brand called Jungalow in 2008 and her first book, *The New Bohemians: Cool and Collected Homes* (2015), was a *New York Times* bestseller. Blakeney has a huge effect and impact on this segment of bohemian-style maximalism: 'I inject as much of myself as I can into my brand so that it can be true to who I am, and stand out in the crowd,' she once said in an interview, adding, 'The only mistake you can really make is to live in a space that doesn't reflect your personality, your desires and your dreams – that's no way to live! I believe that a home should feel comfortable and lived-in.'

Sig Bergamin is yet another contemporary maximalist who takes his own aesthetic to the next level. The Brazilian seamlessly mixes bright colours and motifs that look very much at home together. In his work, and his personal projects, he juxtaposes antique Louis XIV chairs, Indian rugs, floral fabrics, British Colonial-style chairs and hand-painted tiles, for example. Like an expert curator, he takes pieces from different cultures and time periods and blends them together. Eighteenth- and nineteenth-century French and Italian furnishings with modern options from North and South America, for example. He is reportedly so meticulous and particular about his design that he often travels with a duffle bag full of décor objects to customize any hotel, rented space or room on the go.

'Our houses have to be very happy and fun, because what's outside often isn't. People say to me, "Siggy, you mix this pattern with that pattern – and with that carpet?! Why not?"' he told *Architectural Digest* in 2018. His other maximalist essentials? 'A house with no flowers and no books has no life. If you have books you're never alone,' he told *Vogue* in 2018.

right *Justina Blakeney's Jungalow design is seen on a chair in her studio in Los Angeles, California.*

What makes an iconic maximalist interior? As it turns out, there's no one answer, which makes it all the more exciting. Whether or not you focus on a singular aesthetic, there's plenty of inspiration that can be taken from the world's best designers when it comes to over-the-top décor. The only rule of maximalism is that there are no rules. Take, for instance, the highly personal objects, curated small sculptures and keepsakes artfully arranged in the space of Barnaba Fornasetti, which was designed by his father, Piero Fornasetti. It's about personality and total freedom.

Maximalist interiors are also not simply limited to bedrooms or main living areas. The smallest of details can make a bathroom maximalist, for example. But maximalism in the context of public spaces, such as a restaurant, is one of the best examples of opulent, decadent design. Take Sebastian Masuda's Kawaii Monster Café, the once-iconic café in Tokyo

showroom

where oversized strawberries, giant forks and supersized macarons were embedded in the wall. Or Jaime Hayon's art deco dining room at the Standard in Bangkok, with contrasting colours used to powerful effect. Here, we're stepping inside some of the most mesmerizing maximalist rooms around the world to see the secrets of why they work.

opposite *Maximalist doesn't always have to mean clashing prints. Sometimes, it's about choosing one strong focal colour and building out from that As seen in her home here, Susan Hable chose a dense pink that begins with the carpet and carries through to the wallpaper. With inspiring art from different eras, there's an eclectic vibe to the room – plus, the art has touches of the same shades of pink to unite the varied aesthetics. The art deco-style chandelier and fresh florals add a bright touch, while the wood furniture and printed upholstery make the room sing.*

opposite & above *Some of the best maximalist rooms make the eye travel through unexpected vignettes. Originally designed in 1919 by Piero Portaluppi, Casa Atellani in Milan, Italy, was developed by the Castellini Baldissera family. In the entryway, every surface is covered in beautiful details.*

The sculpted busts and dog figures bring life and personality into the space. Elsewhere, shades of forest green permeate through various prints, as well as in statement pieces of furniture, such as the columns. A massive chandelier hanging from the ceiling makes the entire room appear even more grand.

right *Creating a cabinet-of-curiosities-style set-up almost guarantees maximalist euphoria in the home of Barnaba Fornasetti, in Milan, Italy. Originally designed by Piero Fornasetti, Barnaba's father, you can follow the example seen here by curating a beautiful selection of books alongside many different mixed shelves of highly personal objects. Small sculptures, keepsakes, clocks, little mirrors and tiny lamps create a visual journey that speaks to more, more, more. Highly graphic prints by Fornasetti are scattered on rugs, pillows and lampshades for a very layered feeling. Adding prints to the most unlikely of spaces is an easy way to tell a story, and the yellow accent wall creates epic contrast and draws the eye to the curation of objects.*

above & opposite *Lavishly maximalist, just like the famous designer himself, Tony Duquette's Dawnridge is his living estate. With blooming chandeliers, mixed carpets, art hanging from every available surface and plants scattered throughout, it is a maximalist paradise in Beverly Hills, California. Tony and Elizabeth Duquette built Dawnridge in 1949 and began filling it with antiques dating back to the seventeenth century. Today, the space is mainly decorated with a collection of art, sculptures and objects designed by Duquette, as the antiques were sold when the designer passed away in 1999. Despite being entirely grand in appearance, the space is actually quite compact: it was originally only 900 square feet (84 square metres) with a large garden.*

left *Gold and red steal the scene of a living room filled with antiques in the New York apartment of Iris Apfel. The acclaimed eccentric and maximalist tastemaker has millions of followers on social media who flock to her account for her unique viewpoint on all things over the top. Prior to becoming a fashion icon, she had a career in textiles, including a contract with the White House that spanned nine presidencies. Her home is all about her love of colour, texture and ornamentation. The walls are decorated in boiserie panelling. The screen is French, and the chair on the left, covered in Apfel's Old World Weavers tapestry, is seventeenth-century Sicilian. Taking inspiration from a multitude of eras and cultures, the space is as richly decorated and lavish as they way Apfel dresses herself.*

right *The infamous fashion designer Karl Lagerfeld had a Memphis Group design-inspired apartment in Monaco in the early 1980s. There were fantastic sofas in primary colours, cabinets constructed of abstract geometric forms, and certainly no shortage of 1980s shapes. Let there be squiggles and waves ... The bookcases, chairs and lighting fixtures were all equally as statement-making as the next. The industrial floors and white walls allowed that black and white pattern and those primary colours to really shine.*

overleaf *American interior designer Miles Redd shows the power of covering a wall completely in art of all different aesthetics. Then there's also the fact that he plays with scale, opting for paintings of different shapes, sizing and framing, allowing for maximal impact. Rather than using a wallpaper, he's positioned a zebra print screen as the star of the show, standing alongside a red velvet Chesterfield sofa piled with pillows. Much like the artwork, the pillows don't follow convention; they come in all styles, colours, prints and types.*

opposite & above *Since the 1990s, the London-based textile designer Dame Zandra Rhodes has lived in a fantastically pink penthouse that sits above the Fashion and Textile Museum she founded in London. Here, she brings together treasures from some of her favourite travels around the world, which best express her personality and point of view. Chairs are pink and purple, which match the eccentric textile designer's own bright pink hair. Pieces from her friend and fellow designer Andrew Logan are everywhere, and colour, colour, colour rules all. The floor is covered in many hues, from pink to blue and purple. The wide windows and natural lighting keep the space from looking dim or boxed in. The table is decorated like a work of art and mannequins and dresses are integrated into it all.*

left *At the heart of maximalist interior decorating is the pairing of unexpected things. Here, the Victorian-style portraits pair perfectly with the space-age atomic chair and geometric carpet. Designed by Americans Caitlin and Samuel Dowe-Sandes, who run Popham Design, based in Marrakech, Morocco, the polka-dot bedspread and matching curtains are the perfect note that ties everything together in an effortlessly wacky way. The duo call themselves 'pattern-fearless', and that ideology can be seen quite clearly here. White and ivory floral details are integrated throughout the room, lightening up an otherwise intense interior.*

above & opposite *Highlighting individualistic pieces of furniture and lighting, Karim Rashid's work shows that maximalism doesn't always have to rely on more objects. For the most part, his loft in New York is stark, spacing out the few furnishings that defy convention. Focusing on everything retro-futuristic, the neon pink printed walls add an element of 1960s atomic style – and with seating that looks this distinctive, you don't need to do much to make a big splashy statement. Organic shapes and soft lines come together to tie in with the printed walls, and there's no shortage of colour.*

overleaf *Taking inspiration from the darker, moodier look of Victorian times, the interior of Andrew Gn's Paris atelier mixes and matches visually intriguing prints with exotic furniture. Much like the designer's fashion aesthetic, this space lives up to the aesthetic: leopard print and marigold and black stripes act as a neutral. A statement-making chair with Egyptian-inspired features serves as the pièce de résistance. Gold motifs are integrated throughout to create contrast against all the darkness. The densely decorated maximalist space draws from Gothic, Victorian and rococo references.*

opposite & above *Interior decorator Alex Papachristidis brings together the best of old and new, fusing prints on prints with art-like objects in his New York apartment. Here, a dynamic parquet pattern covers the floor while the walls are covered in storybook-like wallpaper. With lots of natural tones and brown hues, the maximalist approach is* *brought to life through a rich aubergine-coloured sofa and chunky gilded chairs. Gold elements and seashell motifs are seen throughout the space, lending a little bit of rococo style. Pops of blue and pink drives a colour conversation that sparks interest but also feels inherently liveable and personal.*

right *Maximalist rooms can be anchored with one unique piece of furniture, as seen in this São Paulo apartment, designed by Joao Mansur. The bold leather sofa in striking burgundy serves as the key to the rest of this room, with dark red accents placed on shades, columns and wall accents. The walls are painted in a light pastel green to juxtapose the deep burgundy. Glamorous elements, such as a crystal chandelier and a silver sculpture, play on the over-the-top looks of design eras from Hollywood Regency to art deco. No surface in the room is left undecorated, with illustrations, paintings and sculptures everywhere.*

left *Tokyo's popular Kawaii Monster Café, founded and designed by Sebastian Masuda, was open from 2015 to 2021. Kawaii (loosely described as the 'culture of cuteness' in Japan) takes maximalism to its kitsch extreme – mixing youthful elements that are cute, happy and fun. Inside the Kawaii Monster Café there were strawberries, giant forks and supersized macarons embedded in the wall. In the centre of the restaurant was a giant, playful merry-go-round, complete with fake dripping icing and a cake-like base, that the lavishly costumed dancers stood on to perform.*

above & opposite *Presented as an exaggerated fantasy take on the decadence and opulence of Hollywood Regency and rococo maximalism, the private club Annabel's in London has become one of the most over-the-top examples of maximalism. Martin Brudnizki Design Studio oversaw the design of the club, at 46 Berkeley Square, in 2018, restoring many of the original features, including the grand cantilevered stone staircase, lavish plaster ceilings and incredible fireplaces. From the gilded mirrors, flowered ceilings, pink marble and crystal lamps, it is the epitome of luxurious, expressive maximalism. Most of the furniture is custom-made, by George Smith, and includes beautifully patterned chairs decked out in pink patterns, fringe, leopard print or velvet details.*

previous page *Inside the Standard hotel in Bangkok is Jaime Hayon's maximalist take on art deco revival. The centre focus of this dining space is the chequerboard print, remixed into different shapes and forms. It's one of the many tried-and-tested ways to create an over-the-top feel without complicating things. The big sunlit windows also help to keep the room bright and not too overly busy. Paired with bright yellow pieces of furniture and simple mid-century modern lighting, it's an op-art lover's paradise that recalls a modern* Alice in Wonderland.

left *Anchoring a room in one colour and creating pattern magic out of it can do wonders for an interior. In Kelly Behun's Park Avenue pied-à-terre, the designer chose a palette of dark blues. She then expanded on the theme with geometric carpeting and graphic walls. Next came a dark blue sofa and a mind-bending striped chair to match the eclectic look of the space. Even the artwork – with its blue, blue sky – matches everything. The only outliers are the rainbow table and the beautiful green tree.*

opposite & above *Mixing together objects that are almost entirely secondhand and vintage, Johnny Carmack has created pink wonderlands through iconic lighting and unique seating arrangements in his Connecticut house. He often sources flower-shaped lamps, pairing them with pink or floral chairs and sofas. With plants and gilded Hollywood Regency details, such as brass mirrors and lamps, all that pink comes together to be quite the statement. Stuffed toys and food-shaped furniture add a kawaii element. Behind the sofa are stacks of frames, proving that art doesn't have to hang on walls.*

right *Pale blue, grass green and deep red come together in harmony in the Florida cottage by Sig Bergamin. The simple space is made incredibly dynamic with all the different styles of seating. With a mission to decorate every surface thoughtfully, pop-art pieces such as illustrations of parrots and portraits unite to showcase personal style. The emphasis of overstuffed pillows provides an element of comfort and, most of all, it's made interesting by the juxtaposition of materials, such as the white-tiled coffee table and unexpectedly cosy throw pillows. The Brazilian designer takes inspiration from his own heritage, colours and his lifestyle and home in Miami.*

opposite *Sasha Bikoff's work on the 2018 edition of the Kips Bay Show House is an example of why you shouldn't forget the stairs. She opted for an all-out explosion of Memphis-inspired motifs, taking references from the 1980s and merging together graphic shapes, lines and waves of all kinds.*

above *No stranger to working exclusively with strong prints, Sasha Bikoff takes an equally dramatic approach in her own home in Greenwich Village, New York, with mixed prints and statement furnishings from the 1980s.*

left *Taking a highly graphic approach, designer Sam Buckley's work plays with colour in a new way to develop his own kind of patterns. Seen here in the Merchiston Crescent home in Edinburgh, Scotland, the large circles painted in dark blue, hunter green, bright yellow, coral, pale pink and burgundy (among others) cover all walls and the ceiling. He then adds an extra layered look to everything by placing mirrors inside the circle motifs, or by matching the carpet to resemble elements from these shapes. Big, green, leafy plants are a hallmark, providing a sense of nature and brightening up the surrounding greens. A yellow lighting fixture hangs in the middle of the room like the sun.*

Even though the only rule is that there are no rules in maximalist interiors, there are certain features that will always lend themselves to being naturally maximalist. Above all else, the element of maximalism to live by is to make your interior feel personal and unrestrained. You can never do too much, and nothing is too over the top. Push the boundaries of art and how you display it – or even what you consider art. Rethink everything. Certain motifs repeat throughout some of the most timeless maximalist interiors, and those are a great place to start if you're looking for inspiration. There's a million and one ways to do the powerful combination of black and white, for example. On the other hand, bold colours and surface decorations can be taken to new heights and extremes.

Consider every space, each surface and all minor details. Nothing is too small to be considered in the world of interior maximalism. And never, ever forget to look up or look down

elements

when you're considering a space. Unique and interesting elements are key to figuring out how you want to design your space. In this chapter, journey down the rabbit hole to discover some time-tested elements that are inherent to maximalist interior design.

opposite *Interior designer Ross Alexander's apartment in Washington Heights, New York. He collaborated with Brock Forsblom to create a maximalist environment where everything has its specific zone to create order and 'every object engages the eye'.*

All About the Art

Let art be the focus of your modern maximalism masterpiece. Choose one centre focal piece that is brilliantly vibrant and expressive, and let it be the main *pièce de résistance* of your room. From there, you can pull out the colours, textures and motifs from this singular piece of art to let it inspire the rest of the room. A well-selected piece of art makes a room come alive with individuality and personal style. From pop art, illustrations, paintings or photography – anything goes.

- Completely cover a wall with art. Neatly arrange the art like tiles in a grid-like procession or mix and match different sizes of art and different styles of frames to create an eclectic vibe.

- Consider the frame as much as the piece of art itself. Seek out colourful or grandly opulent frames. Ornate frames decked out in chunky gold detailing make a big statement.

- Add a screen covered in beautiful painterly florals or patterns – it easily becomes a kind of art form that makes the room feel more interesting and exciting.

- If you're displaying photography, find a common theme to link the images and create a stylized aesthetic. Enlarging your favourite snapshots at a specialist print shop is an instant way to add a deep layer of personalization.

- Sculptures add three-dimensional interest and create a conversation piece. Placing a big cat sculpture in the corner of the room, for example, or a Victorian-style bust on a table is striking. Placing unique photography near a sculpture or bust adds a hint of modern madcap maximalism.

right *A wall of art gives colour, variety and personality to an interior.*

- Add in quirky light fixtures and glass objects. Pair distinctive pop art with black and white photography or animal illustrations to give a sense of layered whimsy.

- Rethink how you display traditional art. Lean a massive, framed vintage poster against the wall on the floor – it's a distinctly casual cool look that's perfect for any maximalist.

- Go grand and devote an entire wall to a large-scale colourful painting or illustration. If you're really feeling bold, ditch the canvas and paint directly onto the wall!

left *An oversized pop-art canvas makes a focal point in a maximalist living room by Sig Bergamin.*

above *A perfectly uniform grid of portraits in the New York apartment of Jonathan Adler and Simon Doonan.*

Black & White

There is no simpler way to make a dramatic impact than with black and white. The dynamic duo pair together perfectly as exact opposites, creating contrast and adding interest to any space. It's the kind of combination that is both witty and fun, adding a surprising hint of movement that shakes up a traditional room and makes it stand out.

- Anchor bright colours with black and white to make them pop. A chequerboard black and white floor is a classic option, but this colour scheme can be integrated into almost any aspect of an interior, such as ceramic tiles in a shower framed by a bright colour.

- Experiment with mixing black and white wallpaper or wall treatments with striped art and diagonal striped flooring for the ultimate maximalist effect.

- Mix and match black and white on your seating. For example, create an op-art space with a black and white striped sofa adorned with black and white pillows with different prints, from animal prints to dots.

right *One of the most famous examples of using black and white in maximalist interiors is seen inside the Greenbrier hotel in West Virginia. A grand entrance is flanked by a stairway with black and white marble flooring. Lush hunter green and lemon yellow are the other colours of choice, which visually pop against the more neutral black and white colour palette. The curtains are draped into a big bow, to add an element of surrealism and fun.*

opposite *Graphically patterned black and white mixes and matches in an array of varieties in this space designed by Kelly Wearstler.*

left *Black and white chequerboard tiles pop against the bold blue and black striped ceramics in a rough-hewn stone-wall outdoor shower in Sorrento, Italy.*

- Think unconventional opposites. Instead of the usual white walls, upgrade them to a dramatic and moody black. You can then use white as a highlight to add dimension and form throughout, within textiles or in furniture pieces.

- Black and white looks especially classic in a kitchen or bathroom. For a more maximalist approach, add in lots of decadent bold and brass fixtures and oddities for a modern *Alice in Wonderland* feel. You could paint your cabinets in a black and white print and frame an accent wall with a big Hollywood Regency style mirror, for example.

- Lean into animal print, like black and white zebra print. Whether it's a vintage ottoman or a rug, it guarantees instant drama.

Bold Colour

Don't be afraid to go wild with bold solid colours: the more unexpected, the better. Imagine a neon pink bedroom or maybe a living room with walls that sing with different colours, such as lime green or canary yellow, set off with a fuchsia pink carpet. Think of colour as a bold act of expression and use it liberally, especially when it comes to walls. With a few statement pieces of furniture and minimal clutter, a bold wall provides a dramatic look that feels bright, clean and confident. Think of every element of the home as an opportunity to experiment with colour.

- Use a vibrant colour on the walls with everything else very pared down. For example, paint the walls of a bathroom bright cherry red, and leave the rest of the room quite bare except for a dramatic mirror and lighting fixture.

- Good, natural lighting is essential when experimenting with revved-up doses of impressive colour. It can keep the room from feeling too boxed in or dim. Any colour goes here – choose what your heart desires in the moment; if you can't commit to a single hue, choose one for each wall.

- Paint vintage furniture in an unexpected colour. For example, take a rococo-style desk and paint it neon pink. As an accent piece, it will instantly stand out in any maximalist room.

right *Bold textiles and bright colours define the Leigh Bowery room at the Hotel Pelirocco in Brighton, England.*

- Pick complementary bold colours, like bright orange and deep blue, to integrate throughout a space. For example, place a mandarin-coloured sofa with a cobalt lounge chair.

- Use white to your advantage. Walls painted a deliciously charged jewel hue look stunning when contrasted with white woodwork or a white ceiling.

- Paint your kitchen cabinets grass green or neon yellow to liven up the space. Then, choose another bright colour to integrate into the scheme – such as turquoise stools or a pink marble countertop.

Surface Decoration

The most maximal of maximalists know to leave no surface behind when it comes to decorating. The ceiling, along with the walls, can be transformed into works of art. Why wouldn't you give the ceiling the same attention you give your walls, after all? And why wouldn't you accessorize your dining room table or coffee table, too? It's all about creating more dimension, whether through applying literal texture through paint, or working with objects.

- Don't forget about ceilings. Hand paint a mural or motif on a ceiling or, if you have a beamed ceiling, paint the beams in a bold colour. The ceiling colours can serve as the palette for your furniture and furnishings.

- Take a cue from Annabel's club (see pages 104–5) and cover an entire bathroom in a frenzy of heavily textured florals or use faux flowers all over one wall. Keep the rest of the room simple and make this the focal point. It's instant maximalism.

- A hand-painted mural is an original and creative way to get a maximalist look. Floral murals go with almost anything and work well with houseplants.

- Make a dining room table the focal point of the room with intricate placemats, cloths, runners and an epic centrepiece. You can change your decoration with the seasons or your mood. Get crafty and build something original using fabric scraps, faux flowers, ribbons and buttons.

right *A hand-painted ceiling by artist David Tremlett utilizes raw brushstrokes with polka-dot motifs. With a minimal glass table by Eric Gizard, it adds an incredibly intimate feeling to a dining room.*

left *Covering an entire bathroom in a frenzy of textured florals is a breath of fresh air in an unexpected space. Keep the rest of the room simple and make this the focus so all the attention goes there.*

opposite *Interior designer Michela Goldschmied's country home in Asolo, Italy, is an explosion of pattern and colour, and a fantastic example of paying attention to all-over surface decoration.*

- Place interesting objects, such as fun vintage toys, sentimental photographs, decorative candles, ceramics and figurines, on a fireplace mantel or bookshelf.

- Plants are a beautiful way to bring in nature and look especially dramatic when grouped together. Cover an entire wall in plants, or hang them all around the perimeter of a room.

- Layer a bold, solid-coloured or pattern-papered wall with unique sconces, masks and candelabras.

- Use dimensional texture paint or stone-effect spray paint to decorate furniture, such as a desk, side table or wooden chair.

Don't Forget to Look Down

The floor is given an equal amount of attention in the maximalist paradise. Whether through floor treatments, printed rugs, carpets, tiles or marble, consider the forms and their texture, colour and feel, and how they mix and match with others in the space. Every time you look down, take it as an opportunity to fill the room with more explosions of colour and pattern.

- Mix stripes with stripes. For example, a striped blue and white rug can be paired with a red and white striped sofa. The practical rug now becomes another element of design.

- Choose an intricately patterned rug as your starting point for your room décor, repeating some of the colours on the rest of your furniture.

- A floral rug livens up a whole room when paired with bouquets in vases or flowering houseplants.

- Colourful staircase runners allow a grand highlight in an unexpected place. If you have wooden or concrete stairs, you could also paint them an unusual, bright colour.

- Animal-print rugs or carpeting are the ultimate maximalist statement. Be bold with leopard or zebra print.

- Geometric rugs can provide a big dose of vintage inspiration. Think psychedelic colours or patterns for a Swinging Sixties feel.

- Go wild with a terrazzo floor! The bigger the pieces and the brighter the colours, the more dynamic it gets.

- Don't disregard vinyl. It's an incredibly easy and affordable way to transform any room. There are plenty of maximalist options that pull bright colours and whimsical prints together. Many of them are inspired by mid-century modern designs.

opposite *A custom-made rug decorates the staircase of an interior by Sasha Bikoff – it is a striking and dynamic way to draw the eye upwards to other parts of the house. The rest of the area is pared back to allow the swirly pattern to make a statement.*

above *A semi-transparent coffee table keeps the floor the focus in a room by Sasha Bikoff.*

- Build your own mesmerizing patterned floors with tiles. There are many wonderful ceramic tiles that combine florals and classic Mediterranean motifs. If it sounds too overwhelming for an entire room, use them as a chic accents in entryways, bathrooms or kitchens.

- Layer floor treatments for extra texture and pattern. Drape a patterned accent rug over a fluffy, bright carpet. Use a small entrance rug on top of ceramic tiles. A dramatic stone or wood floor looks all the more interesting with a special rug to accent it.

opposite *A bold striped rug unites the other elements in a room by Sig Bergmann.*

left *A zebra-print rug in a Hollywood home, by Elizabeth Dinkel Design.*

below *A leopard-print rug and orange velvet Chesterfield daybed make a splash in the New York home of Mary Jane Pool, former editor of* House and Garden.

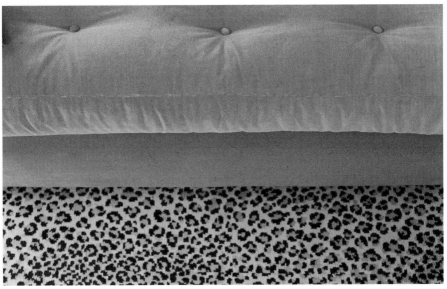

Dramatic Lighting

Finding the right lighting fixture is the key to many maximalist interiors. When looking for inspiration, draw on elements from the opulent eras of the past, including baroque, rococo and art deco. Take a cue from Hollywood Regency and choose gold and brass options with hanging crystals, or feathered standing lamps in plush shades of ivory or blush. Be inspired by the overly glamorous and fanciful. An easy way to find great, unique lighting options is to source them at secondhand shops or head to an antiques market. Think of your lighting as precious objects.

Chandeliers

Look for hanging light fixtures that are expressive in shape, colour or texture. A grand and decadent chandelier never disappoints and adds instant drama to any room. Choose large dangling crystals that reflect light, or crafty, whimsical options made with wire and gems.

Glass & Crystal

Have fun with colour. Coloured glass in shades of vibrant greens, vivid pinks and bold blues highlight a colourful, maximalist room, or choose vintage options in shades of light pink and blue. Beautifully sculpted, colourful Murano glass will always make a bold maximalist statement, while Tiffany-style stained-glass lamps are the ultimate maximalist statement on their own and add a kaleidoscope of colour. Position these lamps as a centrepiece in the space so everyone can see them.

A pair of art deco crystal lamps illuminates a glamorous dark space and gives it a villainous chic look. When using crystal lighting, accent the room with other incredibly glam touches like fresh red roses and Italian marble. Go heavy on the gold and brass finishings.

Novelty Lamps

Fun light fixtures can make a room pop and transform the mood. Keep an eye out for lamps in unusual designs and materials, from flower-shaped lamps to animal-inspired options. They fit in nicely on a mantle, on an end table on a desk, or even on a vanity. Double up and get a pair of matching novelty lamps for an over-the-top symmetrical look.

Printed Lampshades

Look for printed lampshades in fun patterns, colours and textures. Experiment with mixing and matching – a pink glass lamp with a little floral shade for instance. Textures like faux fur and velvet add an extra dose of surrealism.

opposite *An ornate chandelier glows in a deep blue sitting room with a baroque fireplace in an interior by decorator Abigail Ahern.*

Mixed Prints

Add a print or two. Then richly layer on more, more, more. You can never have too many prints in a maximalist space. Think in terms of opposites and add contrast. Play by the rules of the unexpected.

An easy way to make different prints work together is by choosing one overall colour theme, like pink. You can then choose a series of prints that encompass all different shades of pink together. Integrate these prints on the rug, upholstery, pillows, cushions, curtains and wallpapers. Go wild with wallpapers. Choose intricate options like paisley, complex florals, or whimsical examples that riff off animal prints or nature. If you're unsure where to start when it comes to incorporating prints, florals are a very easy solution that flatter any room and come in an endless array of options. Choose a palm-themed wallpaper for example – a maximalist classic – and pair it perfectly with a black and white chequerboard floor for maximal impact. Layer the room with houseplants and cut flowers to connect to botanical prints.

- Choose vases with patterns, or paint your own pots with stripes and dots to clash beautifully with the wallpaper.

- Every surface counts and don't forget to consider the most unexpected places, like the bed, side tables or even little accessories – like porcelain dishes to hold your jewellery – all which can be decked out in a symphony of prints. For example, you could cover a headboard in a cotton chintz print, and choose a toile-print dish or lampshade to go with it.

- Mix primary-coloured stripes, polka dots, chequerboard and geometric forms to achieve a totally different look that riffs on postmodern design or Memphis style. Even in small doses, mixed prints have an epic impact.

- Create richly layered mixed prints through tablescapes. Choose a printed tablecloth and pair it with patterned napkins, embellished forks, hand-painted plates and pretty ceramics.

- Nostalgia is a fun way to play with prints. Think back to the prints you liked as a child and mix and match them.

- Choose graphic pop-art-style prints with linear motifs or organic prints and style them together to get great contrast.

opposite *Layers of patterned Persian rugs, flocked wallpaper and velvet furniture in a neo-Victorian interior in St Benedict B&B, St Leonards-on-Sea, England.*

opposite *A mix of geometric patterns on the floors, staircase and walls, all in a harmonic tonal colour palette, in the Marrakech home of Caitlin and Samuel Dowe-Sands.*

left *Abstract patterns on the floor, furniture and in the art on the walls, in a North Carolina home designed by Ashley Delapp.*

below *A pink and green hand-painted wallpaper in a bold pattern works beautifully with the cotton chintz custom bed in a London interior by Patrick Mele.*

Textiles & Furnishings

Taking a cue from mixed prints, bring textiles in different materials and patterns into your interior. Display wall hangings and tapestries that bring colour and imagination to the room as wall art. Vintage European tapestries bring an Old World feel to a room, or you could also hang an intricate American patchwork quilt or other textile on the wall.

- Choose one pattern style, such as a paisley or floral, and use it on all the furnishings: curtains, lampshades, throws and cushions. Focusing on one powerful pattern through every textile in the room is as bold a statement as mixing and matching prints, if not even more adventurous.

- Layer up on pillows, blankets, quilts and bedding in all kinds of patterns and fabrics that have a commonality of colour, weave or finish, such as satin or matte.

- A one-trick-tip to integrating patterned textiles into your home is to choose a patchwork blanket or quilt. With plenty of pattern and loads of colour, it instantly livens up whatever is near it.

- Choose blankets with interesting and quirky prints and hang them on the wall or fold them across a piece of furniture. Hang one over a metal screen to add pattern and warmth to any room.

- Lean into using textiles in places you might not have thought of yet – like a canopy over a bed, for instance.

- Look for extra-special decorative details. Embroidery, sequins, eyelet, ribbon or tassel trim make textiles even bolder.

- Choose different patterned cushions for a comfy stuffed sofa. It's an easy, small way to start experimenting with patterned textiles and it's also affordable. This is a commitment-free way to try the look too. Change out your pillows every week or switch them up with your mood or the season.

- DIY it. Tie dye or shibori dye bed sheets, a duvet cover or a custom cotton wall hanging. Any patterned furnishings you make yourself feel instantly more individual and personal.

opposite *Blue and grey toile and geometric patterns unite a variety of textiles and furnishings in a Matthew Monroe Bees-designed bedroom.*

opposite *Jenny Kee's vivid prints, rugs and cushions decorate the bedroom of her Blue Mountains home in Australia.*

above *A monochrome colour palette allows for variation in patterns and textiles to achieve the ultimate understated maximalist look.*

Found Objects & Quirky Vignettes

Reinterpret everything and rethink anything when you're going for the maximalist look. This is a look that thrives off individuality, and one way to get that is by accumulating found objects and placing them in a way that creates wonderful whimsical vignettes. This is the ultimate conversation starter in any home, and one of the easiest ways to add a strong injection of personality to a space.

Head to endlessly inspiring antique stores or flea markets for rare, one-of-a-kind oddities. Choose from vintage toys, antique trays, outdoor signs, painted music boxes and anything else that captures your imagination. Look for street signs, statues, old carnival decorations or things you'd never think of including in a conventionally traditional décor.

- Start small with one piece, such as an animal-shaped clock or a vintage license plate. A McDonald's sign against traditional wallpaper adds a bit of humour and irony. Neon light-up signs can be placed in a formal living room to create a fun and unique look that speaks for itself.

- Work with what you have. Maybe you love fashion and collect shoes, bags and jewellery. Rather than hiding these pieces in the back of your closet, put them on display. A colourful, embellished pair of high heels on the mantle, or rare, beautiful bag on a bookcase. An animal sculpture could be bedecked with jewellery, or fairy lights put up to frame a mirror.

- Give objects the space they deserve. Don't clutter them too much, or they may get lost. Make sure they shine bright and act as a statement in the room.

- Choose a theme. Maybe you like pigs or cats, and you could focus all your found objects around those animals.

- Blend practicality and whimsy. A novelty clock or a cat-shaped landline telephone serve purpose but add art.

- Mix your heart's wildest desires: clown statues, cake-shaped ceramic boxes, a horse-shaped chalkware clock, vintage Depression-era glass trays. It's all about what you love and what makes you happy.

opposite *A porcelain dog statue is decorated with jewellery by Begüm Khan.*

above *A neon design by Phil Oakley creates a focal point while richly patterned fabrics add vibrancy.*

opposite *Found objects and curiosities are displayed in a birdcage cabinet that adds whimsy and eccentricity to a room.*

left *Look for elaborate and unusual picture or mirror frames; this one creates an unexpected accent against a brick warehouse wall.*

below *Put your favourite collections on display. Here ornate handbags and jewellery decorate a wall and side table in an interior by Andrew Gn.*

Statement Furniture

Maximalist interiors are the perfect excuse to scoop up that eccentric piece of furniture you've been eyeing. Whether it's a yellow and black striped sofa with tassels and lacquered wood or an Egyptian Revival-style bench and matching chairs, nothing is too extravagant. Seek out furniture that speaks to you and makes a wild statement about what you love. Think in terms of unique shapes, colours and motifs. An ultra-plush, tufted, overstuffed granny-style sofa can be considered a piece of statement furniture in the right interior. Sometimes you don't need a lot to make a maximalist statement. It's not always about cluttering the space with things – so an eccentric piece of statement furniture can do the job of standing in as the main star of the show while making everything else flow around it. Anchoring the room with one wild piece creates drama.

If you have more than one piece of statement furniture per room, it's fun to create contrast between different styles and aesthetics. Maybe you own a Hollywood Regency coffee table but have a Victorian fainting sofa. Think of bringing these different worlds together to create something that feels eccentrically new.

- Create a statement piece. Replace, repaint or re-cover neutral furniture with bright, colourful options – a pink sofa, for instance, or a neon green desk. Look for bold shades of colour, such as cherry red or robin's egg blue, to give furniture instant character. Gold trimming and deep, shiny lacquer can be added to pre-existing furniture to make a statement.

- Even a small piece can be a starring object. Hand-painted wood chests or side tables can become the focal point, depending on how extravagant the piece is.

- Chairs with intricate woodcarvings, rococo features or opulent embroidery can also transform a room. Think of your furniture as big pieces of art and examine the details.

- Highlight maximalist furniture with equally stand-out accessories, whether that be eclectic touches or bric-a-brac all elegantly placed on top.

- Rethink materials: play with glass, Lucite, brass and iron. Different materials and textures can come together to make your furniture statement-worthy.

- Seek out pairings. A pair of wild chairs or two matching side tables covered in animal print make twice the statement, while keeping the space symmetrical.

opposite *A colourful butterfly chair and hanging light make a powerful statement against an all-white backdrop.*

index

ABOUT THE AUTHOR

Kristen Bateman is a maximalist New York City-based writer, editor and creative consultant. She also writes for the *New York Times*, *Vogue*, *W* magazine, *Architectural Digest*, *Elle* and many other magazines. Her focus is on writing about interiors, fashion history, culture and beauty. She also has her own jewellery brand, Dollchunk. Other books by Kristen include *The Little Book of Tom Ford*, *The Met Gala Lookbook* and *The Little Book of New York Style*.

PICTURE CREDITS

The publishers would like to thank the following for their kind permission to reproduce the images in this book.

AKG Images VIEW Pictures/Peter Cook 57. **Alamy** Elizabeth Whiting & Associates 44, 45; A. Astes 64; Andreas von Eisiendel 143; Andriy Blokhin 34–5; Associated Press 38–9; Diego Grandi 32–3; Elizabeth Whiting & Associates 31t; Eugen Wais 13; Frederic Reglain 65, 102–3; funkyfood London – Paul Williams 11; Hemis 25b; imageBROKER. com GmbH & Co. KG 9, 12; MET/BOT 17/Neil Setchfield 19; Perry van Munster 16; Piero Cruciatti 61; stockeurope 14–5; STOCKFOLIO 48–9; The Picture Art Collection 21; Victor Watts 51; WENN Rights Ltd; Zefrog 31b. **Ashley DeLapp Interior Design** 135, 145t. **Bridgeman Images** 26–7, 50; Alastair Carew-Cox 23; Christie's Images 25t, 37, 59; NPL – DeA Picture Library Pictures Library/D. Balzaretti 24; G. Dagli Orti/NPL – DeA Picture Library 28b; Philadelphia Museum of Art, Pennsylvania, PA, USA/Gift of Collab: The Group for Modern & Contemp. Design 58; Prismatic Pictures 20; San Francisco Museum of Modern Art 63. **Getty Images** Slim Aarons 54–5, 66–7. **Haydon Studio** 106–7. **Hotel Pelirocco** 128–9. **Interior Archive** Annie Schlechter 35 (Dorothy Draper), 119 (Ross Alexander, Brock Forsblom), 124–5 (Dorothy Draper), 126 (Kelly Wearstler), 130 (Matthew Bees), 139b (Mary Jane Pool), 147 (Matthew Bees); Bernard Touillon 127 (Marco De Luca); Graham Atkins-Hughes 141 (Abigail Ahern), 153t (Abigail Ahern); James McDonald 68 (Martin Brudnizki), 104 (Martin Brudnizki), 105 (Martin Brudnizki); Joanna Maclennan 152 (Fabienne Collombel); Karyn Millet 139t (Elizabeth Dinkel Design); Luke White 151; Mark Luscombe-Whyte 132–3 (Eric Gizard Associates), 150 (Begum Khan); Miguel Flores-Vianna 72 (Luke Edward Hall, Duncan Campbell), 145b (Patrick Mele); Stefano Scata 134 (Michela Goldschmied). **John Bessler** 2, 6–7. **OTTO Archive** Jenna Peffley 74–5 (designed by Justina Blakeney); Roger Davies 84–5 (designed by Iris Apfel); Scott Francis 52–3 (designed by Mario Buatta). **Regina Spelman** Jacques Schumacher 86–7. **Richard Powers** 4–5, 43, 71, 77, 78, 79, 80–81, 82, 83, 88–9, 92–3, 94, 95, 96–7, 98, 99, 100–1, 108–9, 112–3, 121, 123, 138, 144, 148, 149, 153b, 155. **Sasha Bikoff Interior Design** Chris Mottalini 115, 136, 137; Nick Sargent 114; Patrick Cline 131. **Shutterstock** Horst P. Horst/Condé Nast 40–1, 47. **Studio Sam Buckley** Alix McIntoch Photography 116–7. **Unsplash** Steph Wilson 120–1. **Vintage Show Pony** 110, 111. **Wikicommons** /L'Illustration 28t. **Zandra Rhodes** Bridie O'Sullivan 90, 91.

First published in 2024 by OH
An Imprint of HEADLINE PUBLISHING GROUP

1 3 5 7 9 10 8 6 4 2

Cataloguing in Publication Data is available from the British Library

Hardback ISBN 978-1-83861-223-8

Printed and bound in China

HEADLINE PUBLISHING GROUP
An Hachette UK Company
Carmelite House
50 Victoria Embankment
London EC4Y 0DZ

OH Publisher: Lisa Dyer
Desk editor: Matt Tomlinson
Design: Lucy Palmer
Production: Arlene Lestrade

www.headline.co.uk
www.hachette.co.uk